Sentences

A **complete sentence** must name a person, place, or thing and then tell what happens. A **complete sentence** begins with a capital letter and ends with a punctuation mark.

The children played all day.

Read the groups of words below.
Draw a circle around the **complete sentences**.
Then match the sentences with the pictures they tell about.

1. running through the park with the dog

2. Toby ran as fast as he could

3. Kim and her friends

4. The girls won the game

5. The friendly dog

6. The dog wagged his tail happily

Complete Sentences

Put a **capital letter** at the beginning of the complete sentences.
Put a **period** at the end of the complete sentences.
Cross out the other groups of words.

1. $\overset{S}{\cancel{S}}$ally had fun at the park .

2. watched football all afternoon

3. dad and Mom and the children

4. everyone woke up early in the morning

5. all the way to the beach

Use two of these phrases to make complete sentences.

all the children	ate pizza
later that night	went to bed
John and his friends	it rained

1. _____

_____

2. _____

_____

Subject and Predicate

Every sentence has two main parts:
       subject - tells <u>who</u> or <u>what</u> the sentence is about
       predicate - tells what the subject <u>does</u>

Draw a line under the **subject** and a circle around the **predicate**.

The long train moved slowly through the tunnel.

1. Everyone in the class cheered.

2. Our Mothers took us on a picnic.

3. The police took care of the people.

4. Jose fed the cat and dog.

5. The horses ran quickly through the field.

6. The teacher liked my story.

Subject and Predicate

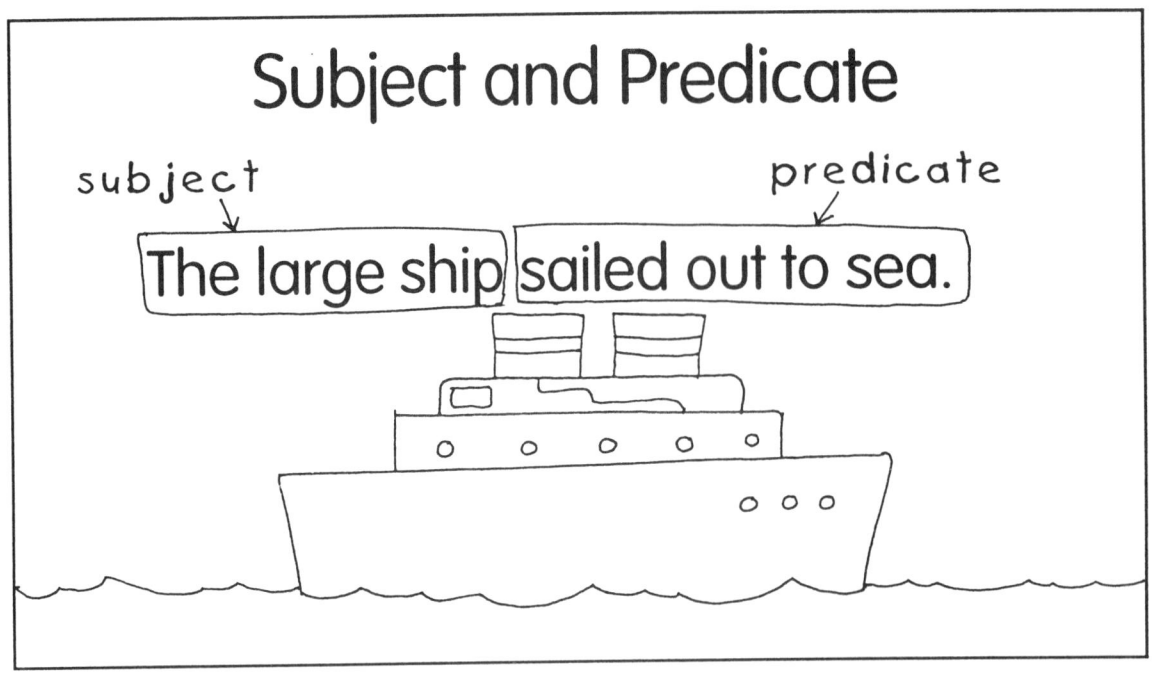

subject → The large ship | predicate → sailed out to sea.

Write **subject** by the part that tells **who or what the sentence is about**.
Write **predicate** by the part that tells **what the subject does**.

predicate   1. liked to play jump rope

_____   2. Israel and his friends

_____   3. The frogs

_____   4. hopped around the **backyard**

_____   5. Clara's uncle David

_____   6. gave us money for sodas

_____   7. read a story about a spider

_____   8. The teacher

4

Subjects

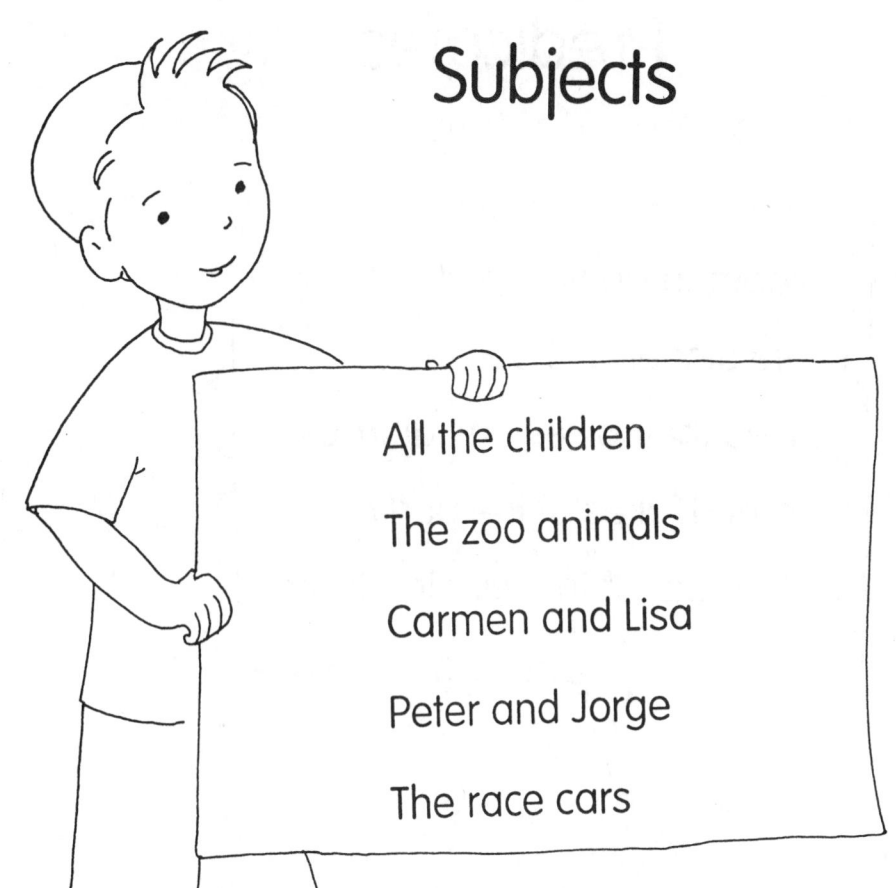

All the children

The zoo animals

Carmen and Lisa

Peter and Jorge

The race cars

Write one of these **subjects** on each blank below to make a complete sentence.

1. _____ drove through the rain.

2. _____ shared their lunches.

3. _____ won the game.

4. _____ enjoyed the play.

5. _____ slept in the sunshine.

Predicates

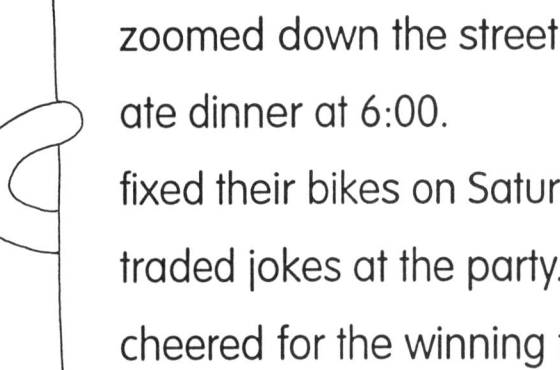
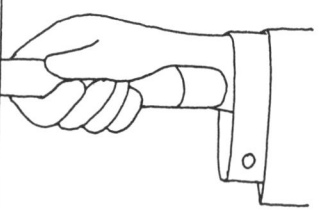

zoomed down the street.

ate dinner at 6:00.

fixed their bikes on Saturday.

traded jokes at the party.

cheered for the winning team.

Write one of these **predicates** on each blank below to make a complete sentence.

1. Alison and Manuel _fixed their bikes on Saturday_

2. The shiny, red bike _____

_____

3. Aunt Helen _____

_____

4. We _____

_____

5. They _____

_____

Nouns

A **noun** is a word that names a **person**, **place**, or **thing**.

Circle the nouns in these sentences.

1. The (boy) ate an (apple,) a (banana,) and a (sandwich.)

2. Give the coat to that student beside the white building.

3. Have you ever been to the river outside the city?

4. The bus was late one day this week because of the storm.

5. Three little giraffes live on the plains in Africa.

6. The swift train ran down the tracks to my town.

Proper Nouns

Proper nouns name special **persons**, **places**, and **things**.
Proper nouns always begin with a capital letter.

Mr. Gomez   **Michigan**   **Colorado River**

Circle the proper nouns in these sentences.

1. What kind of car does your (Aunt Mary) drive?

2. Jennifer and Jerome live in a brick house on Allman Street.

3. Lake Kivu is a large lake in eastern Africa.

Write a proper noun for each noun below.
Don't forget the capital letters.

girls   Susan and Sarah

a park   _____

a school   _____

a teacher   _____

children   _____

a television show _____

One and More Than One

Some nouns name one person, place, or thing.

house   **school**   **toy**

Some nouns name more than one person, place, or thing.

houses   **schools**   **toys**

Read these nouns that name one thing.
Add an **s** to each word to make it name **more than one**.

tree	trees
river	
flower	
boat	
pencil	
store	
rose	
cracker	

Find the Nouns

Circle all the nouns you can find in the puzzle below:

```
C H I L D R E N X T O Y A P P L E D
A B O A T O G I P O T E C S P K P R
F G U M E R E R A M Z A L A I S E E
R U B U S O E A P G O R A N R K N S
I C O A T S S T E A M S S D J A Y S
C D O G S E E D R M G B S W I T O E
A O K I S S C O T E A E L I F E Q S
B A N A N A O F R I E N D C O N Z W
O W S I P O U C H M I C E H X T P O
Y H O U S E N E S T M H R I V E R M
S U N L N S T O R M T E A C H E R A
L A K E F U R C I T Y S R O O X E N
S C H O O L Y H O S P I T A L C U P
```

Check each word as you find it in the wordsearch.

Africa	cup	lake	sandwich
apple	dog	life	school
banana	dresses	mice	seed
benches	fox	nest	skate
boat	friend	oxen	son
book	fur	paper	storm
boys	game	pen	sun
children	geese	pot	teacher
city	gum	pouch	teams
class	hospital	ram	toy
coat	house	rat	woman
cot	jay	river	year
country	kiss	roses	

Challenge: Can you find other words in the puzzle?

10

Pronouns

Pronouns are words that take the place of nouns.

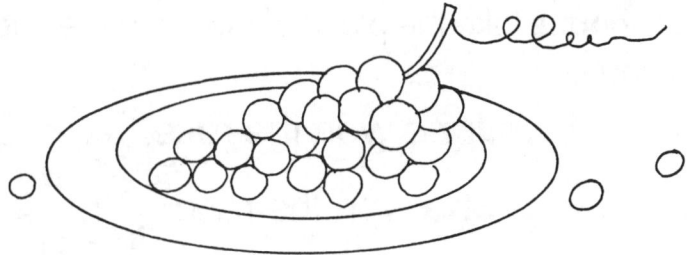

Joanna gave the **grapes** to **George.**

She gave **them** to **me**.

Read the sentence pairs below.
Underline the nouns and draw a circle around the pronouns.

1. The <u>waves</u> sparkle brightly.

   (They) sparkle brightly.

2. Tom and I finished quickly.

   We finished quickly.

3. Teri likes to play outside.

   She likes to play outside.

4. Later the teacher went for a walk.

   Later he went for a walk.

Pronouns

Some **pronouns** take the place of nouns in the subject part of the sentence.

Jane won the race.

She won the race.

Write the **pronoun** that can take the place of each underlined **noun**.

_____ 1. <u>Andy</u> may take the bear home today.

_____ 2. <u>The dinner</u> of chicken and potatoes was delicious.

_____ 3. <u>The animals</u> in the zoo were glad to see Mike, Carlos, and Tony.

_____ 4. <u>Mr. Lee</u> walked down the street to the corner.

_____ 5. <u>Rosa and I</u> are going to Bob's party.

_____ 6. <u>Gina</u> ran to the park to meet her friends.

| I | you | he | she | it | we | they |

Pronouns

Some **pronouns** take the place of nouns that come after a verb.

The teacher read **the class** a story.

The teacher read **them** a story.

Write a **pronoun** to take the place of each underlined **noun**.
Here are some object pronouns you might use:

me	you	him	her	it	us	them

them 1. Please pass the potatoes.

_____2. Nat invited Jane to come home with him today.

_____3. The zoo ranger won't let us feed the wild animals.

_____4. Dad gives the map to Mom when we travel.

Use each of these **pronouns** in a sentence. | **us** | **them** | **her**

_____

_____

_____

_____

13

Verbs

Verbs tell what someone or something does.

The horse **ran** across the field.

Underline the **verbs** in the sentences below.
Some sentences will have more than one **verb**.

1. The chorus sang their songs perfectly last night.

2. We laughed and cried during the movie.

3. Everyone finished the work early and then played games.

4. The bunny hopped around the yard to find his dinner.

5. Last Tuesday our class took a field trip.

6. The children sang "Happy Birthday" to Mary.

7. I went shopping at the mall yesterday.

8. Bingo ran to the garden and dug a hole.

The Verb "To Be"

The verb **to be** joins the subject of the sentence with words that describe it. The **to be** verb has many forms.

be	**am**	**is**
are	**was**	**were**

We **are** playing after school.

The storm **was** wild and windy.

Underline the **to be** verbs in the sentences below.

1. All my neighbors are friendly and polite.

2. The Main Street School team was the best in the area.

3. The sandwiches and the cookies were tasty.

4. Were you at the party on Saturday?

5. I am always happy to see my grandmother.

6. The sun is shining and the birds are singing.

Helping Verbs

have has had

These verbs help the main verb tell what someone or something does.

The students **have** finished their work.

Underline the **helping verbs** in the sentences below.

1. Mr. Stevens <u>had</u> baked a cake for the party.

2. My teacher has read a story every day this week.

3. The bees have taken the nectar from the flowers.

4. The players had won all their games all year.

5. Pete and Ted have finished their homework.

Write a sentence using one of the helping verbs.

_____

_____

_____

_____

Verb Word Search

Circle each **verb** you can find in the puzzle below.

```
C T W I N B C L I M B T T Q A W E R E B
R O Q C T R R I D E K O H S Z Q I P E L
I O B U T O W B P H W O R W C X W A S O
E K H T Q U A R E A G E O A A N F T T W
D Q A V G G T I Q D X R W Q R D X A W L
A F S P X H C N P A S S H S R R G E J G
B E Q N H T H G S K I P H Z Y P H K D S
V L C H E E R P H K T I L K G M E E P B
T L W A L K E D S K A T E P L A Y D C A
S W I M V G L R A N L W F H Y J I I A K
L A U G H E I I E Q K A V B R O K E T E
R O D E M Q K Q G O E V U Y H A V E C I
V D J R H K E M A K E E F G J R R V H G
R G F R E E Z E R O Z D J T J U M P T W
I A G K L C O O K E D Q P U L L M N I S
F R N I P P S D R I V E M O O W G X E F
```

Cross out each word as you find it in the word search.

bake	cut	like	swim
blow	drive	make	talk
bring	fell	pass	throw
broke	freeze	pat	tie
brought	go	play	took
carry	had	pull	walked
catch	has	ran	was
cheer	have	ride	watch
climb	help	rode	waved
cooked	jump	skate	were
cried	laugh	skip	win

17

Adjectives

An **adjective** describes a noun.
It tells **how many** or **what kind**.

We took **three yellow** flowers to the **birthday** party.

Draw a circle around the **adjectives** in the sentences below.

1. The (busy) street seemed to be filled with (fast) cars.

2. The poor, old woman walked slowly down the dark path.

3. Ira ate three fresh berries and some crusty French bread.

4. Jay was the only boy from a small school in the big band.

Write two sentences with adjectives.
Try to use more than one adjective in each sentence.

1._____

_____

2._____

_____

Adjectives

Use these clues to complete the puzzle on page 20.

Across

1. The _____ sky looked peaceful.
4. We won the _____ game we played.
7. The rose is a _____ flower.
8. The _____ ice cream tasted great.
9. The giraffe has a _____ neck.
10. I have _____ one nose.
11. The _____ class was too big for the room.
12. Do you like yellow apples or _____ ones?
13. The _____ story made us cry.
15. "What a _____ idea," said my friend.
16. The youngest puppy was _____ than the others.

Down

1. Paul had the _____ piece of cake.
2. Spaghetti is my favorite _____ food.
3. The _____ story made us laugh.
4. Troy had _____ fries with his hamburger.
5. The holidays are a _____ time.
6. I try to be a _____ person all the time.
10. My _____ shirt is soft and comfortable.
13. The _____ kitten begged for milk.
14. A race car goes very _____ .
17. Mother gave me _____ orange in my lunch.

Adjectives

Use the clues on page 19 to help you complete this puzzle.

Word Box

an	fast	old
beautiful	first	only
biggest	friendly	red
blue	French	sad
busy	Italian	silly
cold	large	small
crazy	long	smaller

Capitalization

Every sentence begins with a **capital letter**.

The pizza was good.

My mother picked me up after school

Where are you going?

Look at the sentences below.
Circle the words that should have **capital letters**.

1. (the) class was sad when their teacher moved away.

2. a horse with brown spots ran across the hills.

3. jonah and Melanie finished their work on time.

4. everyone wanted to go to the beach on Saturday.

5. does it rain every day in a rainforest?

6. come over after school and play with me.

7. pete has a new pet mouse.

8. how fast can you swim across the pool?

Punctuation

Every sentence ends with a **punctuation mark**.

a period   The cake tasted good**.**

a question mark   Did you enjoy the cake**?**

an exclamation point   That was the best cake ever**!**

Read the sentences below and write the correct punctuation mark for each one.

1. Did you bring your lunch today ?

2. All of the lunches were in paper bags

3. Don't do that

4. Haven't you finished your lunch yet

5. What a great surprise

6. Were you late for school

7. The funny clowns made me laugh

8. How old are you

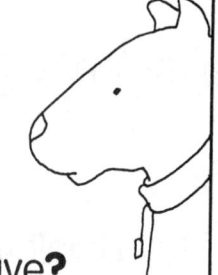

Run-on Sentences

Think about where one sentence
ends and a new sentence begins.

My dog is a poodle. **W**hat kind do you have**?**

How should these sentences be separated?
Put a **capital letter** at the beginning of each sentence.
Put a **punctuation mark** at the end of each sentence.

    H   S

1. have you seen my cat? she is gray.

2. is that a cat no, it is a skunk

3. bob can't find his cake did Ann eat it

4. why did you miss school were you sick

5. do you like to play ball i think it is fun

6. did you go to the zoo i went on Monday

7. pick up those toys put them away

8. is Dad home yet i need to talk to him

23

Correct these Sentences

Put a **capital** at the **beginning** of each sentence.
Put a **punctuation** mark at the **end** of each sentence.

1.   W
   when did you get that toy? ^Ccan I play with it?

2. they must go home at 4:30 what time is it now

3. grandma is coming today she will stay a week

4. how old are you i am 10

5. i am going to the movies can you come

6. john has soup for lunch what do you have

7. don't climb that tree it isn't safe

8. i like that picture will you draw me one

Correct this Story

1. Read the story.
2. Capitalize the sentences.
3. Punctuate the sentences.

help i can't get away

i am trapped in this net will help come

soon how will I escape it's no fun to be in a

net i want to be back in the water

what is that it is a rip in the net can I get

out that way the rip isn't big will I be able to

push my way out i'm going to try here I go

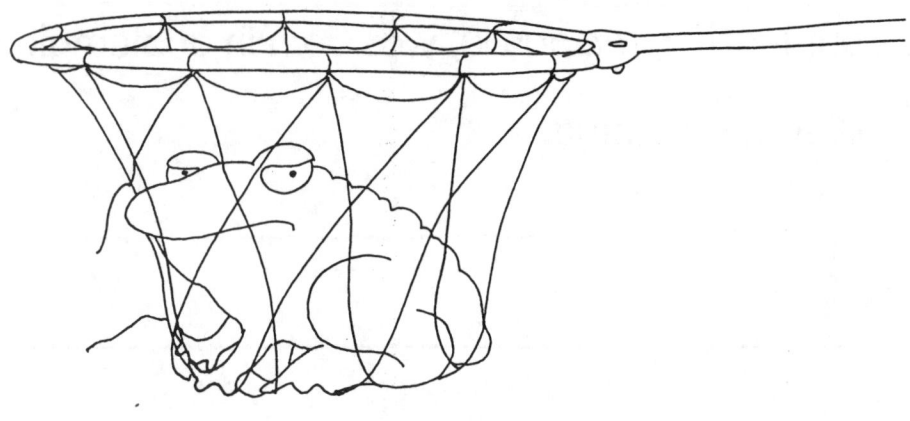

Using Capital Letters

Always use a **capital letter** with:

- **proper nouns and the pronoun I**
  (names of certain people, places, and things)
  Maria, **N**ebraska, **I**
- **titles**
  Mr. Bill Davis, **D**r. Susan Smith
- **days, months, and holidays**
  Tuesday, **A**pril, **T**hanksgiving **D**ay
- **cities, states, counties, countries**
  Denver, **T**exas, **N**orth **C**ounty, **M**exico

Circle the words in the sentences below that need capital letters.
Write the sentences putting in the capital letters.

1. my cousin teresa lives in mobile, alabama.

   _____

   _____

2. mark said, "i want to go to san francisco for thanksgiving."

   _____

   _____

3. our teacher, mr. garcia, was born in guatemala and now

   lives in oklahoma.

   _____

   _____

Punctuating Abbreviations

Use a period after titles for abbreviations:
doctor - **Dr.**
professor - **Prof.**
reverend - **Rev.**

Remember to punctuate these titles too:
Ms. Mrs. Mr.

Add periods where they are needed.

1. The pastor of our church is Rev Davis.

2. Dr Hernandez took my temperature to see if I had a fever.

3. Take all your science projects to Prof Ortega's classroom.

4. After the picnic, Mr Adams took the children to the zoo.

Write two sentences using title abbreviations.
Don't forget to use capital letters and periods.

1. _____

_____

2. _____

_____

Commas

Use **commas** between the name of a city and a state or a province.

Little Rock, Arkansas

Put commas where they belong:

1. Memphis Tennessee

2. Atlanta Georgia

3. Anchorage Alaska

4. San Francisco California

5. Salt Lake City Utah

6. Antler Lake Alberta

Write where you live here:

_____

Use **commas** between the day and the year.

June 7, 1995

Put commas in these dates.

1. April 1 1993

2. October 15 1966

3. March 15 1948

4. July 4 1776

5. January 1 1995

6. December 25 1993

Write your birthday here:

_____

Commas in a Series

Use **commas** between items that come **in a series**:

apples, pears, and bananas

Put commas in these sentences.

1. I like to play with my friends Jim Bob and Tom.

2. Pablo has pet cats dogs and fish.

3. We ate pizza with cheese pepperoni and onions on my birthday.

4. We played on the swings slide and bars in the park.

Write a sentence containing a series of at least three things.

_____

_____

_____

_____

Parts of Speech

Review

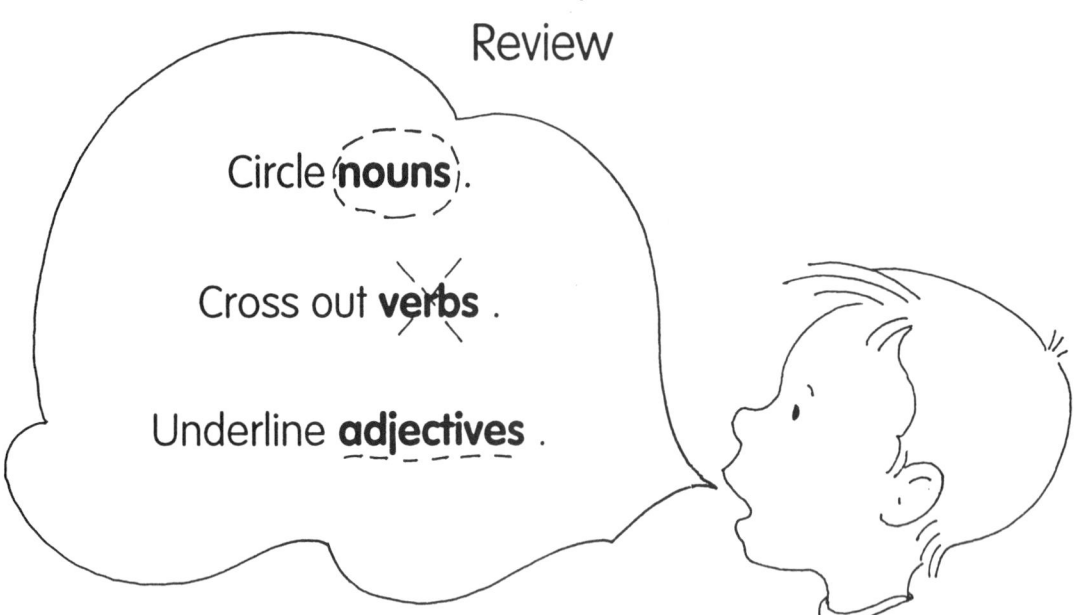

Circle **nouns**.

Cross out **verbs**.

Underline **adjectives**.

food	flower	jump
carry	fast	purple
purse	men	strong
cute	sing	hike
drive	tree	catch
happy	wet	family
climb	bicycle	sad
tall	build	school

Answer Key

Please take time to go over the work your child has completed. Ask your child to explain what he/she has done. Praise both success and effort. If mistakes have been made, explain what the answer should have been and how to find it. Let your child know that mistakes are a part of learning. The time you spend with your child helps let him/her know you feel learning is important.

page 1

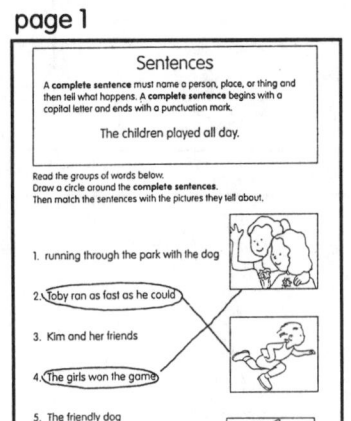

Sentences

A **complete sentence** must name a person, place, or thing and then tell what happens. A **complete sentence** begins with a capital letter and ends with a punctuation mark.

The children played all day.

Read the groups of words below.
Draw a circle around the **complete sentences**.
Then match the sentences with the pictures they tell about.

1. running through the park with the dog
2. Toby ran as fast as he could
3. Kim and her friends
4. The girls won the game
5. The friendly dog
6. The dog wagged his tail happily

page 2

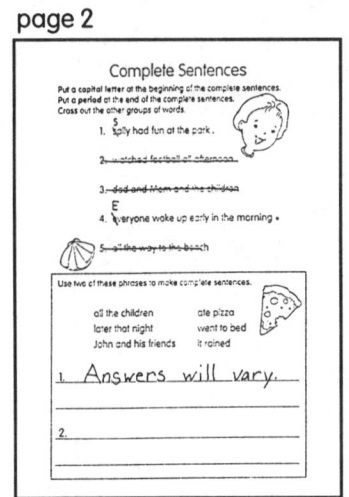

Complete Sentences

Put a capital letter at the beginning of the complete sentences.
Put a period at the end of the complete sentences.
Cross out the other groups of words.

1. Sally had fun at the park.
2. watched football at afternoon
3. dad and Mom and the children
4. Everyone woke up early in the morning.
5. all the way to the beach

Use two of these phrases to make complete sentences.

all the children	ate pizza
later that night	went to bed
John and his friends	it rained

1. Answers will vary.

2. _____

page 3

Subject and Predicate

Every sentence has two main parts:
  subject - tells **who** or **what** the sentence is about
  predicate - tells what the subject **does**

Draw a line under the subject and a circle around the **predicate**.

<u>The long train</u> moved slowly through the tunnel.

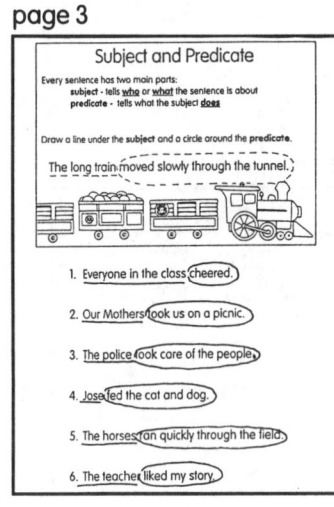

1. Everyone in the class cheered.
2. Our Mothers took us on a picnic.
3. The police took care of the people.
4. Jose fed the cat and dog.
5. The horses ran quickly through the field.
6. The teacher liked my story.

page 4

Subject and Predicate

subject   predicate
The large ship sailed out to sea.

Write subject by the part that tells who or what the sentence is about
Write predicate by the part that tells what the subject does

predicate 1. liked to play jump rope
subject 2. Israel and his friends
subject 3. The frogs
predicate 4. hopped around the back yard
subject 5. Clara's uncle David
predicate 6. gave us money for sodas
predicate 7. read a story about a spider
subject 8. The teacher

page 5

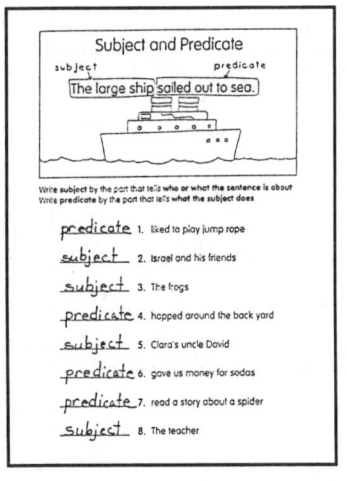

Subjects

All the children
The zoo animals
Carmen and Lisa
Peter and Jorge
The race cars

Write one of these subjects on each blank below to make a complete sentence.

1. Answers _____ drove through the rain.
2. will _____ shared their lunches.
3. vary. _____ won the game.
4. _____ enjoyed the play.
5. _____ slept in the sunshine.

page 6

Predicates

zoomed down the street.
ate dinner at 6:00.
fixed their bikes on Saturday.
traded jokes at the party.
cheered for the winning team.

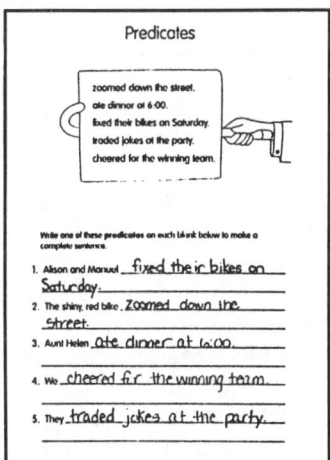

Write one of these predicates on each blank below to make a complete sentence.

1. Alison and Manuel fixed their bikes on Saturday.
2. The shiny, red bike zoomed down the street.
3. Aunt Helen ate dinner at 6:00.
4. We cheered for the winning team.
5. They traded jokes at the party.

page 7

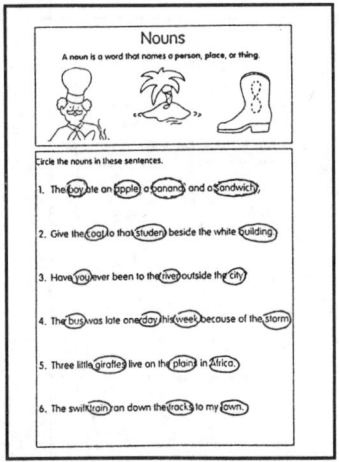

Nouns

A noun is a word that names a **person, place, or thing.**

Circle the nouns in these sentences.

1. The boy ate an apple, a banana, and a sandwich.
2. Give the coat to that student beside the white building.
3. Have you ever been to the river outside the city?
4. The bus was late one day this week because of the storm.
5. Three little giraffes live on the plains of Africa.
6. The swift train ran down the tracks to my town.

page 8

Proper Nouns

Proper nouns name special persons, places, and things.
Proper nouns always begin with a capital letter.

Mr. Gomez   Michigan   Colorado River

Circle the proper nouns in these sentences.

1. What kind of car does your Aunt Mary drive?
2. Jennifer and Jerome live in a brick house on Allman Street.
3. Lake Kivu is a large lake in eastern Africa.

Write a proper noun for each noun below.
Don't forget the capital letters.

girls   Susan and Sarah
a park   Answers will vary.
a school   _____
a teacher _____
children   _____
a television show _____

page 9

One and More Than One

Some nouns name one person, place, or thing.
  house   school   toy

Some nouns name more than one person, place, or thing.
  houses   schools   toys

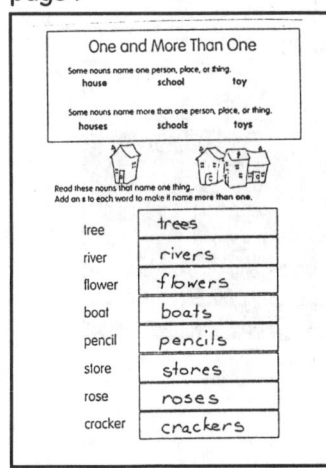

Read these nouns that name one thing.
Add an s to each word to make it name more than one.

tree	trees
river	rivers
flower	flowers
boat	boats
pencil	pencils
store	stores
rose	roses
cracker	crackers

page 10

Find the Nouns

Circle all the nouns you can find in the puzzle below:

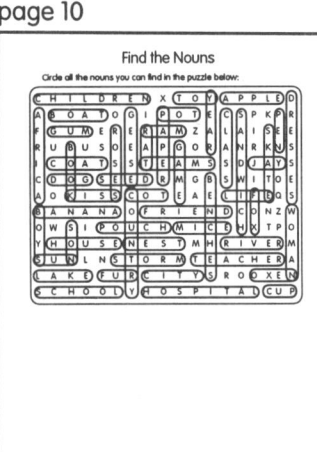

page 11

Pronouns

Pronouns are words that take the place of nouns.

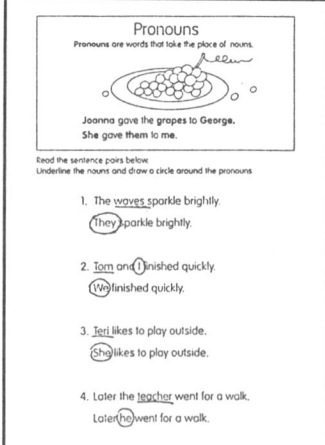

Joanna gave the grapes to George.
She gave them to me.

Read the sentence pairs below.
Underline the nouns and draw a circle around the pronouns.

1. The <u>waves</u> sparkle brightly.
   (They) sparkle brightly.

2. <u>Tom</u> and (I) finished quickly.
   (We) finished quickly.

3. <u>Teri</u> likes to play outside.
   (She) likes to play outside.

4. Later the <u>teacher</u> went for a walk.
   Later (he) went for a walk.

page 12

Pronouns

Some pronouns take the place of nouns in the subject part of the sentence.

Jane won the race.
She won the race.

Write the pronoun that can take the place of each underlined noun.

he 1. <u>Andy</u> may take the bear home today.

it 2. <u>The dinner</u> of chicken and potatoes was delicious.

they 3. <u>The animals</u> in the zoo were glad to see Mike, Carlos, and Tony.

he 4. <u>Mr. Lee</u> walked down the street to the corner.

we 5. <u>Rosa and I</u> are going to Bob's party.

she 6. <u>Gina</u> ran to the park to meet her friends.

| I | you | he | she | it | we | they |

page 13

Pronouns

Some pronouns take the place of nouns that come after a verb.

The teacher read the class a story.
The teacher read them a story.

Write a pronoun to take the place of each underlined noun.
Here are some object pronouns you might use:

| me | you | him | her | it | us | them |

them 1. Please pass <u>the potatoes</u>.

her 2. Nat invited <u>Jane</u> to come home with him today.

them 3. The zoo ranger won't let us feed <u>the wild animals</u>.

it 4. Dad gives <u>the map</u> to Mom when we travel.

Use each of these pronouns in a sentence. | us | them | her

Will vary!

page 14

Verbs

Verbs tell what someone or something does.

The horse ran across the field.

Underline the verbs in the sentences below.
Some sentences will have more than one verb.

1. The chorus <u>sang</u> their songs perfectly last night.

2. We <u>laughed</u> and <u>cried</u> during the movie.

3. Everyone <u>finished</u> the work early and then <u>played</u> games.

4. The bunny <u>hopped</u> around the yard to <u>find</u> his dinner.

5. Last Tuesday our class <u>took</u> a field trip.

6. The children <u>sang</u> "Happy Birthday" to Mary.

7. I <u>went</u> <u>shopping</u> at the mall yesterday.

8. Bingo <u>ran</u> to the garden and <u>dug</u> a hole.

page 15

The Verb "To Be"

The verb to be joins the subject of the sentence with words that describe it. The to be verb has many forms.

| be | am | is |
| are | was | were |

We are playing after school.
The storm was wild and windy.

Underline the to be verbs in the sentences below.

1. All my neighbors <u>are</u> friendly and polite.

2. The Main Street School team <u>was</u> the best in the area.

3. The sandwiches and the cookies <u>were</u> tasty.

4. <u>Were</u> you at the party on Saturday?

5. I <u>am</u> always happy to see my grandmother.

6. The sun <u>is</u> shining and the birds <u>are</u> singing.

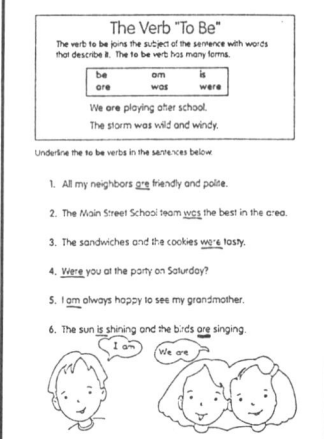

page 16

Helping Verbs

| have | has | had |

These verbs help the main verb tell what someone or something does.
The students have finished their work.

Underline the helping verbs in the sentences below.

1. Mr. Stevens <u>had</u> baked a cake for the party.

2. My teacher <u>has</u> read a story every day this week.

3. The bees <u>have</u> taken the nectar from the flowers.

4. The players <u>had</u> won all their games all year.

5. Pete and Ted <u>have</u> finished their homework.

Write a sentence using one of the helping verbs.

Will vary.

page 17

Verb Wordsearch

Circle each verb you can find in the puzzle below.

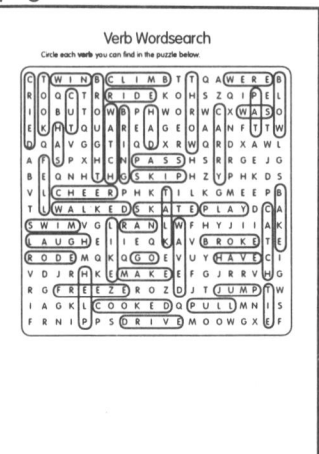

page 18

Adjectives

An adjective describes a noun.
It tells <u>how many</u> or <u>what kind</u>.

We took three yellow flowers to the birthday party.

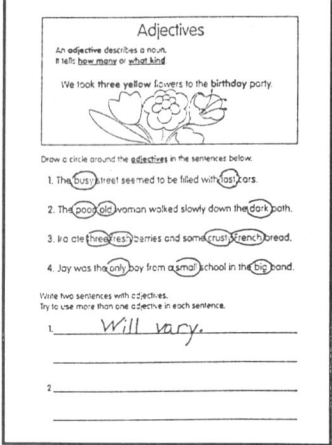

Draw a circle around the adjectives in the sentences below.

1. The (busy) street seemed to be filled with (fast) cars.

2. The (poor) (old) woman walked slowly down the (dark) path.

3. Ira ate (three) (fresh) berries and some (crusty) French bread.

4. Jay was the (only) boy from a (small) school in the (big) band.

Write two sentences with adjectives.
Try to use more than one adjective in each sentence.

1. *Will vary.*

2.

page 20

Adjectives

Use the clues on page 26 to help you complete this puzzle.

page 21

Capitalization

Every sentence begins with a capital letter.

The pizza was good.
My mother picked me up after school.
Where are you going?

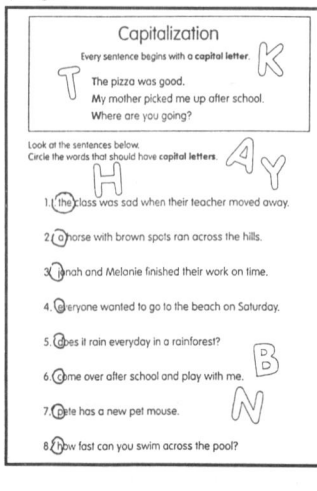

Look at the sentences below.
Circle the words that should have capital letters.

1. (the) class was sad when their teacher moved away.

2. (a) horse with brown spots ran across the hills.

3. (Jonah) and Melonie finished their work on time.

4. (everyone) wanted to go to the beach on Saturday.

5. (does) it rain everyday in a rainforest?

6. (come) over after school and play with me.

7. (Pete) has a new pet mouse.

8. (how) fast can you swim across the pool?

page 22

Punctuation

Every sentence ends with a punctuation mark.

a period	The cake tasted good.
a question mark	Did you enjoy the cake?
an exclamation point	That was the best cake ever!

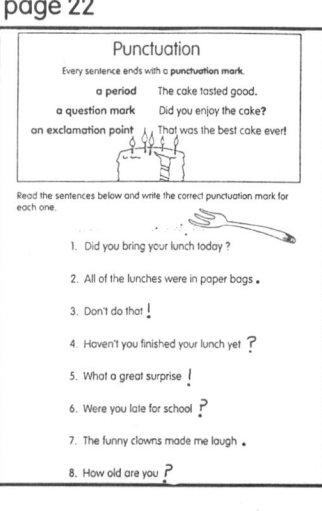

Read the sentences below and write the correct punctuation mark for each one.

1. Did you bring your lunch today ?

2. All of the lunches were in paper bags .

3. Don't do that !

4. Haven't you finished your lunch yet ?

5. What a great surprise !

6. Were you late for school ?

7. The funny clowns made me laugh .

8. How old are you ?